DUCK HUNTING

BY BLAKE POUND

BELLWETHER MEDIA · MINNEAPOLIS, MN

Jump into the cockpit and take flight with Pilot books. Your journey will take you on high-energy adventures as you learn about all that is wild, weird, fascinating, and fun!

This edition first published in 2013 by Bellwether Media, Inc.

No part of this publication may be reproduced in whole or in part without written permission of the publisher. For information regarding permission, write to Bellwether Media, Inc., Attention: Permissions Department, 5357 Penn Avenue South, Minneapolis, MN 55419.

Library of Congress Cataloging-in-Publication Data

Pound, Blake.
 Duck hunting / by Blake Pound.
   p. cm. – (Pilot books: outdoor adventures)
 Includes bibliographical references and index.
 Summary: "Engaging images accompany information about duck hunting. The combination of high-interest subject matter and narrative text is intended for students in grades 3 through 7"–Provided by publisher.
 ISBN 978-1-60014-797-5 (hardcover : alk. paper)
 1. Duck shooting–Juvenile literature. I. Title.
 SK333.D8P68 2013
 799.2'44–dc23   2012000961

Printed in the United States of America, North Mankato, MN.

TABLE OF CONTENTS

In the Blind 4

Clothes, Dogs, and Gear 8

Planning and Safety 16

Louisiana:
  Duck Capital of America 20

Glossary 22

To Learn More 23

Index 24

IN THE BLIND

In the early morning on a cool fall day, a flock of ducks flies through the sky. They search the wetlands below for a good place to land and feed. Nearby, two hunters sit in a blind. With their dogs beside them, they wait for the ducks to fly closer. One of the hunters uses a wooden duck call to attract the birds. The ducks glide toward the water. The hunters raise their guns and take aim. They have only a few seconds to take their shot!

Duck hunting is a challenging sport. Hunters spend hours outdoors in pursuit of their prey. They do not mind cold weather or wet clothes. They are willing to hike long distances to reach good hunting grounds.

Ducks are intelligent birds with sharp senses. In order to be successful, duck hunters must scout wetlands before hunting season begins. The shores of rivers and lakes are the best places to start. Hunters find out where ducks like to nest and feed. They study duck habits and learn to think like ducks. They also search for the perfect spots to set up their blinds. When fall comes, they are ready to hunt!

CLOTHES, DOGS, AND GEAR

Duck hunters need to wear the right clothing when they go out to bag birds. Warm, insulated clothes help hunters stay comfortable in cool fall weather. Waders keep them dry as they make their way through wetlands. Camouflage helps hunters blend in with their surroundings.

Bird dogs are important to any successful hunt. They help hunters locate and flush ducks. They also retrieve ducks that hunters have shot from the sky. Hunters spend a lot of time training their bird dogs to be calm and patient. A restless dog can scare birds away and ruin a hunt.

Types of Bird Dogs

Retrievers
Dogs that find and retrieve birds that have been shot down

Flushers
Dogs that find birds and drive them into the open so hunters have clear shots

Pointers
Dogs that find birds and point their heads and bodies toward them

9

duck call

Hunters use duck calls to attract ducks. Most calls are made of wood and have a small reed inside. The reed vibrates when the hunter blows into the call. Some hunters use their hands and mouths to mimic the sounds of ducks. Ducks move toward the sounds out of curiosity.

Duck hunters also use decoys to lure ducks close. Decoys are made of wood or plastic and are painted to look like real ducks. Hunters set up decoys close to their blinds. They place them where they can be seen from the sky.

Some hunters attach strings to their decoys so they can make them move. Decoys that dip their heads look like ducks that are feeding. Other hunters have started to use roboducks. These mechanical decoys dip their heads and flap their wings on their own. They allow hunters to keep constant watch on the sky.

roboduck
decoy

Duck hunters use shotguns to bring down their prey. They load the shotguns with **cartridges**. Each cartridge holds **gunpowder** and small pellets called shot. When a hunter pulls the trigger, the shot spreads out quickly over a wide area. This gives the hunter a better chance at hitting a flying duck than if he or she used a single bullet.

cartridges

Hunters can choose from different kinds of shotguns. Pump-action shotguns load a cartridge when the hunter pumps the gun. Semi-automatic shotguns can fire a single cartridge every time the trigger is pulled. Double-barreled shotguns have two barrels that fire one cartridge after the other.

Hunters can go after ducks in a couple different ways. In pass shooting, hunters study the flight patterns of ducks. This helps them learn where the ducks fly when going from one body of water to another. Pass shooters stay in blinds on dry ground and wait for the ducks to fly overhead. Then they stand up, take aim, and fire.

Other hunters prefer jump shooting. They follow the shore of a river or lake and sneak up on ducks in the water. When the ducks fly into the air, the hunters take aim and fire.

PLANNING AND SAFETY

Duck hunters must know and follow state hunting laws. All states require hunters to purchase a license. They also set specific dates for the hunting season. Ducks can usually be hunted only when they migrate in the fall. Hunting is not allowed in the spring when ducks breed and raise their young.

During duck hunting season, each state sets a limit on the number of birds a hunter can kill each day. Within these limits, only a certain number of each species can be taken. By following these laws, hunters help keep duck populations strong.

Orange for Safety

Some states require hunters to wear blaze orange when they walk to their hunting spots. This bright color makes them visible to other hunters.

Hunters should not shoot at ducks that are out of range. This is called "skybusting." It often only wounds ducks or scares them away from other hunters.

Responsible hunters follow a code of conduct. They keep a safe distance from one another and move away from other groups in the area. They never shoot at ducks that approach another hunter's blind.

Hunters must also take care of the environment. They should not leave any equipment or trash behind when they move off their hunting grounds. This keeps the area clean and ready for other hunters. Many hunters join groups that conserve wetlands. They work hard to maintain wildlife habitats and ensure that others will have ducks to hunt.

LOUISIANA: DUCK CAPITAL OF AMERICA

Southern Louisiana is a duck hunting hot spot between November and January. Hundreds of freshwater marshes line the coast along the Gulf of Mexico. Mallards, pintails, and other ducks gather here in the winter.

The small town of Gueydan, Louisiana sits directly on an important duck flyway and is known as the Duck Capital of America. Each fall, the farms of Gueydan attract thousands of migrating ducks. Their fields provide the ducks with plenty of food and shelter. The town hosts a duck festival the weekend before Labor Day to celebrate the sport of duck hunting.

Gueydan

GLOSSARY

bag—to shoot down and capture

bird dogs—dogs trained to help hunters find and retrieve birds

blind—a small, hidden shelter where duck hunters hide and wait for ducks to appear

camouflage—clothing with coloring and patterns that blend in with the surroundings

cartridges—shells that contain everything needed to fire shot from a shotgun

code of conduct—a set of rules that establishes how a person should behave; hunters follow a code of conduct to respect one another and the land.

conserve—to protect; hunters conserve duck habitats so they will always have somewhere to hunt.

decoys—life-like models of ducks; hunters use decoys to attract ducks.

duck call—a noisemaker that mimics the sounds a duck makes; duck calls are used to attract ducks.

flush—to chase out into the open from a place of hiding

flyway—a specific route that birds fly when they migrate

gunpowder—a mixture of substances that explodes when ignited

insulated—made with materials that trap heat; hunters wear clothes that are insulated to keep warm.

license—a document that gives legal permission to do an activity

migrate—to move from one place to another, often with the seasons

reed—a thin piece of wood, metal, or plastic in a duck call that vibrates when a hunter forces air over it

scout—to explore an area to learn more about it

waders—waterproof pants that cover duck hunters from their feet to their waists

TO LEARN MORE

At the Library

Carpenter, Tom. *Waterfowl Hunting: Duck, Goose, and More.*
Minneapolis, Minn.: Lerner Publications, 2013.

Omoth, Tyler. *Duck Hunting for Kids.* North Mankato, Minn.:
Capstone Press, 2013.

Truax, Doug. *A Good Day for Ducks.* Memphis, Tenn.: Ducks
Unlimited, Inc., 2003.

On the Web

Learning more about duck hunting
is as easy as 1, 2, 3.

1. Go to www.factsurfer.com.

2. Enter "duck hunting" into the search box.

3. Click the "Surf" button and you will see a list
of related Web sites.

With factsurfer.com, finding more information
is just a click away.

INDEX

bird dogs, 4, 8, 9
blinds, 4, 7, 11, 14, 19
cartridges, 12, 13
clothing, 8, 16
code of conduct, 19
conservation, 19
decoys, 11
duck calls, 4, 10
Duck Capital of America, 20, 21
fall, 4, 7, 8, 16, 20
jump shooting, 14
laws, 16
license, 16
limits, 16
Louisiana, 20, 21
migration, 16, 20
pass shooting, 14
safety, 16, 19
scouting, 7

shotguns, 4, 12, 13
skybusting, 19
species, 16, 20
wetlands, 4, 7, 8, 19, 20